Until I Change

Affirmations for Mastering Personal Change

Inspirations and Illustrations by

Charlotte D. Grant-Cobb, PhD

Until I Change

Affirmations for Mastering
Personal Change

All Rights Reserved © 2002-2010 by RICHER LIFE, LLC

╫RICHER Publications

For information address:
RICHER LIFE, LLC
4600 E. Washington Street, Suite 300
Phoenix, Arizona 85034
www.richerlifeassociates.com

First Edition: December 2002

Illustrations By: Charlotte D. Grant-Cobb, PhD

Printed in the United States of America

ISBN: 978-0-9744617-0-0

Dedication

This book is dedicated to those people who are willing to embrace each new season of change with a willing heart and an open mind.

Introduction

The changes that occur around us, and to us, often trigger in us an overpowering desire to retreat rather than to evolve.

This is the paradox of personal growth.

In my coaching practice, I work only with people who are willing to get to core -- to examine their personal truth – and then to evolve. By bringing renewed awareness to the process of change, we are able to replace old behaviors and inappropriate motives with intentional choices.

The affirmations in this book are meant to help you meet the challenge to live your life with conscious intention. The inspirations recognize that the source for uncovering your promise rests within you.

Nothing changes until I change is a personal truth that has led me to walk with confidence, while respecting all others who share this planet with me. May these words encourage you through each season of change.

Until I Change

Nothing changes until I change.

When I change, everything changes.

3

Reflections...

I will experience my life through the gifts of spirit, truth and love.

Reflections...

My freedom to choose wisely is absolute.

Reflections...

Until I Change

Right or not, desired or denied, my presentation affects outcomes.

9

Reflections...

I will have the presence of mind and strength of character to say "no" even to a good idea, if it distracts me from my purpose.

Reflections...

Until I Change

I am responsible for my peace and happiness. Even so, I recognize that my energy is infectious.

13

Reflections...

I can speak my mind without fear, because my mind stays centered in gentle thoughtfulness.

Reflections...

Until I Change

It takes as long as it takes.

Reflections...

Until I Change

When I am mindful of my thoughts, truths fall gently from my mouth.

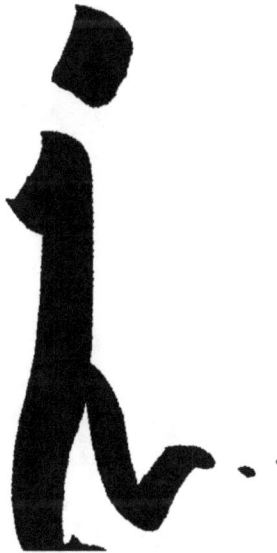

Reflections...

Until I Change

Ready or not,
tomorrow will come.

Reflections...

Until I Change

I become what I do by learning
from what I have done.

There is no separation.

Reflections...

Until I Change

New thoughts take root
during transitions.

Reflections...

Until I Change

I witness my past behavior with clarity and adjust appropriately.

Reflections...

Until I Change

*I make better choices when
I hear all my options.*

29

Reflections...

Though I cannot control what happens within me, I can always control what happens around me.

Reflections...

Until I Change

I will not allow my future to
become a victim of my past.

Reflections...

Transitions give me time to practice, experiment and explore.

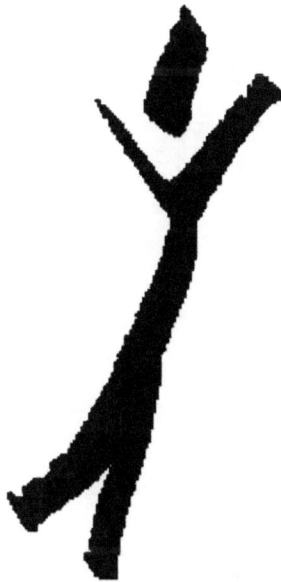

Reflections...

Until I Change

It is the frequency of my correct choices, and the repetition of my correct behaviors that bring me closer and closer to my desired outcomes.

Reflections...

Until I Change

Through every transition and season,
I will rejoice.

Reflections...

*Being a good companion is
sweeter than being right.*

Reflections...

The greatest challenge is a cluster of barriers connected by a single thread.

Reflections...

*Each experience provides me with
one perfect moment to enjoy.*

Reflections...

Preparation is the practice of learning from the patterns of successful people.

Reflections...

Until I Change

I take care of the ones I love.

Reflections...

When I courageously witness my own behaviors, I know what to do next.

Reflections...

Until I Change

I will take the time to complete the
work required to find my personal
truth.

Reflections...

Until I Change

To be a good singer, I must sing.

Reflections...

My personal truth cannot be altered, no matter the circumstance.

Reflections...

My body is a gem that I must cherish.

Reflections...

My comfort is expendable.
My freedom is not.

Reflections...

*I make my choices intentionally
to avoid unintended consequences.*

Reflections...

Until I Change

I count it all joy when my mind is centered on peace, tranquility and serenity of spirit.

Reflections...

Until I Change

I see each moment as it is, instead
of the way someone else taught me
it should be.

Reflections...

Practice enables speculation without penalty.

Reflections...

New knowledge demands that I examine old filters.

Reflections...

I practice daily the skills needed to take my next steps.

Reflections...

Until I Change

The place that I am in is the result
of my cumulative choices.

Reflections...

Until I Change

Discernment comes through practice.

Reflections...

Until I Change

Any day is the best day to start.

79

Reflections...

*I have decided to openly receive
the love another freely shares.*

Reflections...

Mindfulness, sifted through every communication, diffuses intention.

Reflections...

*The quality of my life is the result
of my cumulative choices.*

Reflections...

I recognize that arriving too early for a healthy relationship is as hopeless as staying too late for a poor relationship.

Reflections...

With an open mind, I am open to more.

Reflections...

I am the one who gives meaning to my life.

Reflections...

*I cannot expect to achieve
perfection in the midst of planning
and practicing.*

93

Reflections...

Until I Change

The time spent in between the
beginning and the end is the
transition.

95

Reflections...

*I find great joy in
expressing my love
creatively.*

Reflections...

Until I Change

Before I share my opinion,
I will center my mind.

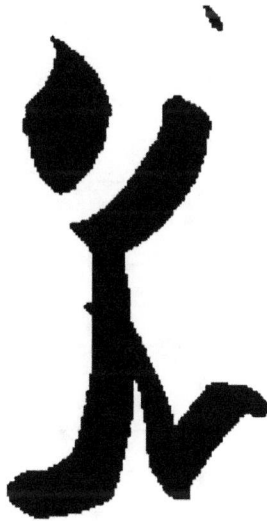

Reflections...

I know when to move to the next thing because I pay attention to everything.

Reflections...

My word is the manifestation of my integrity.

Reflections...

My gifts link me to like-minded people.

Reflections...

Until I Change

*I greet each new day with
new hope and genuine joy.*

Reflections...

*I will leave others with their self-esteem,
no matter the tenor of the exchange.*

Reflections...

In times of conflict, I recall the place of serenity where I last knew balance.

Reflections...

I recognize the truth when I see it, hear it and feel it.

Reflections...

My commitment to the ones I love supersedes my commitment to things I love.

Reflections...

Until I Change

My denial of the facts does not change reality.

Reflections...

I will be the first to go when it is time.

Reflections...

Until I Change

My choices are cumulative.
My behaviors are iterative.

121

Reflections...

Until I Change

Someone is waiting for me to arrive.

Reflections...

Until I Change

When it's time, it's time.

Reflections...

Until I Change

Someone is waiting for me to arrive.

Reflections...

Until I Change

129

Until I Change

www.ingramcontent.com/pod-product-compliance
Lightning Source LLC
LaVergne TN
LVHW051415080426
835508LV00022B/3092